THE GREAT TEXAS SCARE
A STORY OF THE RUNAWAY SCRAPE

THE
GREAT TEXAS SCARE
A STORY OF THE RUNAWAY SCRAPE

by
Martha Tannery Jones

Illustrated by
Donna Loughran

Hendrick-Long Publishing Co.
DALLAS

DEDICATION

To my parents, Clifton and Ruby Tannery

A special thank-you to Karen Navratil who
encouraged me to write this book

Library of Congress Cataloging-in-Publication Data

Jones, Martha.
  The great Texas scare.

  Summary: When fighting breaks out in Texas in 1836, the
approach of the Mexican army forces Manda and her family to flee
their home and seek refuge in the open countryside.
  1. Texas—History—To 1846—Juvenile fiction. [1. Texas—
History—To 1846—Fiction. 2. Frontier and pioneer life—Fiction]
I. Loughran, Donna, ill. II. Title.
PZ7.J7217Gr 1988   [Fic]   88-767
ISBN 0-937460-31-1

© 1988 Martha Tannery Jones
Illustrations © 1988 Hendrick-Long Publishing Co.

Design and Production:
Dodson Publication Services, Austin, Texas

Hendrick-Long Publishing Co.
Dallas, Texas 75225

CONTENTS

CHAPTER 1

NEIGHBORS

"Where are we going?" asked Manda.

"You'll see!" Jane replied.

Manda followed as Jane led the way across the Tanner farm. The girls walked up to a rail fence enclosing a grassy field. Inside the fence stood a huge bull.

"This is Terror," Jane said. "We just got him, and my father paid a lot of money for him. He's mean—real mean, but I'm not afraid. See, I'll show you!"

Manda gasped at what she saw next.

Jane climbed over the fence and started toward Terror. She picked up some rocks and began throwing them at the bull. When one hit his side, he stopped eating and raised his head. Jane took a few steps backward.

Terror went back to his meal, and Jane's courage returned. She scooped up some clods of dirt and again headed in his direction. Every so often, she pitched one near him.

From behind the rails, Manda watched. *That bull*

probably isn't mean at all, she thought. *Jane just said that to make herself look brave. Still, he might be more dangerous than she knows.*

"That's enough, Jane," Manda called, "I know how brave you are. Come on back. Let's go see what the boys are doing."

"In a minute, Manda. I haven't hurt him yet," Jane yelled. "Are you scared?"

"No, but you should be," Manda yelled back.

Jane laughed and threw a large clump of hard earth. It hit Terror on the head. He looked at her and snorted. With one foot he began to paw the ground. Jane made a face at him. She put her thumbs in her ears and waved her fingers. The bull charged!

Jane ran as fast as she could toward the fence. Just before she reached the safety of the pine rails, Terror caught up with her. He lowered his head and then raised it. He hooked Jane's skirt on his horns.

As Jane tumbled over the fence, a big piece of her skirt was ripped away. Terror shook the material off his head and bellowed loudly. Then he ran off in the other direction, much to the relief of the girls.

"That was a narrow escape!" Manda said. "But your skirt is torn. What is your mother going to say?"

"I'll think of something to tell her," Jane said as she tossed her head to make her red braids fall down her back.

The two girls watched the boys play ball for a while. Then they went to a clump of pine trees where they

often played. They worked for over an hour making a
pine straw house. They swept up the dry tan-colored
pine needles with their hands, carefully leaving the red
soil beneath. They scraped it into lines to stand for the
walls of a small room. Then they added more rooms

until they had bedrooms, a parlor, and a grand ball-room. They stood back to admire their work.

Manda and Jane liked to pretend. In reality, they had never even seen a home so magnificent.

Ten-year-old Amanda Katherine Barker, "Manda" for short, lived in a house made of logs. It had two rooms connected by a covered but open porch. In one room her parents slept. In the other, which served as the main living area, Manda had a narrow bed across from the fireplace. At night, her two brothers climbed a ladder nailed against the wall to sleep in the loft. Michael was sixteen, and Patrick, who was called "Padrac," was only three.

Manda's father, James Barker, had brought his family to Nacogdoches two years ago. Manda remembered when they lived in Tennessee, Papa was always telling stories he heard about Texas. He said a man could get rich because land was plentiful, and the fertile soil made the crops grow. But Manda had heard Mama say, "Papa has a roaming spirit. He has fast feet!"

Mama had finally agreed to move to the Texas territory that belonged to Mexico. Manda knew Mama, too, had a hankering to see what was over the next hill.

The nearest neighbors, the Tanners, lived about a mile from the Barker farm. They had settled at the same time as the Barkers, and the two families had become good friends. The Tanners had two children. Jeffrey had just turned five, and Jane Ellen was ten, like Manda. The father, Charles, was a doctor. Mrs. Tanner held school for some of the children in the area. She taught the lessons in her home whenever her students didn't have planting or picking or other chores to do.

It was the end of June, 1835.

All of a sudden, Jane's brother Jeffrey ran under the pine trees, kicking pine straw in all directions. He quickly destroyed their house. Jane ran after him, but she couldn't catch him.

"Jeffrey, I hate you! I'm telling Mama," she screamed. "Why did you tear up our house? I'll get you for this!"

"I'm a storm. I'm a bi-i-ig storm with a strong wind," he yelled back. Jeffrey ran around waving his arms but keeping his distance.

About that time, Mrs. Tanner came from the house and walked toward the children. Jeffrey ran off through the pines when he saw her coming.

"Mama, Jeffrey ruined everything! You make him stay away from us," Jane whined.

Mrs. Tanner ignored Jane's demand and asked sternly, "Jane Ellen, do you know what happened to my syrup cookies? I uncovered the plate and it's empty."

Jane's expression changed from a pout to a look of innocence. "Yes, Mama," she said. "I think I just might know. Yesterday, during our lessons, I do remember seeing crumbs on Jeffrey's chin."

"I can't believe he could have eaten the whole plateful!" cried Mrs. Tanner. "But they're gone! Now I have nothing to serve the women who've come to my quilting bee."

With a quick look around to make sure Jeffrey couldn't hear, Jane continued. "Well, I can't imagine why he did such a thing! But I saw him playing around the table where you put them. I had that bad coughing spell and had to keep going to the bucket for water."

"Well, he knows better. I'm surprised he didn't get sick," Mrs. Tanner said, turning to go.

A smile played at one corner of Jane's mouth and she said sweetly, "Yes, Mama."

Manda noticed Jane had been careful to keep her backside, and the torn skirt, out of her mother's sight.

Jeffrey ran by laughing, and Jane stuck her tongue out at him and said, "You just wait! You'll be sorry later!"

Manda looked down at the scattered pine needles and remembered how the day before Jane had gone again and again for water, each time coughing loudly. Suddenly Manda thought, *Why, Jane ate those cookies herself, and now she's blaming her little brother.*

"Jane, you shouldn't have—" Manda began. But she was interrupted by shouting that seemed to come from the cornfield. Manda thought something terrible must have happened. Then she realized what she heard were shouts of joy.

Shading her eyes with her hand, Manda saw Jane's

father running toward the house. She could not hear what he was saying, but she saw two men on horseback riding away.

"Come on, Manda," Jane cried. "Let's go find out what the excitement is about."

As the girls neared the house, they saw that all the women had left the porch to gather around Dr. Tanner. Manda stood by her mother, Katie Barker, and listened.

"Mr. Marsh and Joe Nolan just told me about some trouble down in Anahuac," Dr. Tanner said. "William Travis and twenty-five men have forced a Mexican captain and his troops to leave Texas."

Shaking her head, Mrs. Tanner said, "More fighting! Where will it break out next?"

"Who knows? It can happen any place where there are Mexican soldiers and unhappy Texans," Dr. Tanner said.

"We have no voice in our own affairs," one of the women shouted. "The Mexican government doesn't understand us."

"Well, we won the fight at Anahuac, but one of the reasons it started was that we learned more troops are being sent here to keep us in line," said Dr. Tanner.

Manda felt herself shiver in the summer heat. All the talk of war with Mexico scared her. She didn't want Papa and maybe Michael to leave home to go fight. Manda reached up and took her mother's hand. As she held it, she knew Mama was thinking the same thoughts.

While driving home in the buggy that afternoon, Mama turned to Manda and said, "I figure your father has heard about Anahuac."

Manda didn't want to think about the trouble between Texas and the Mexican government. So she changed the subject, saying, "I wonder what Papa and the boys did in town today."

Mama laughed and said, "I imagine it took both your father and Michael to keep up with that little brother of yours."

"You're right, Mama," Manda agreed. "Padrac can be a stinker!"

"We should never have started calling him by that nickname," Mama said. "Just because *he* says his name that way is no reason why the rest of us couldn't say Patrick."

"But Padrac suits him," Manda said. She had no intention of calling her three-year-old brother by such a grown-up name as Patrick.

They smelled it before they turned down the dusty road that led home—skunk!

"Oh, my!" Mama said. "That varmint must be close. I wonder what stirred it up."

"I don't know," said Manda, holding her nose. "But I hope it doesn't smell like this at home—and we're almost there!"

As the buggy drew closer to the Barker home, the awful odor grew stronger. And Manda and Mama heard Padrac screaming.

CHAPTER 2

A VISIT FROM SAM HOUSTON

Mama urged the horse to go faster. When they pulled to a stop in the yard, they saw a strange sight. Padrac stood by the well, stripped of all his clothes, yelling as loudly as he could. A lather of lye soap covered his body. Manda's father, with a handkerchief tied over his nose, held up a bucket of cold well water and poured it over his small son. Soap and water streamed down Padrac's sides and formed a puddle around his feet.

"James, what happened?" Mama cried.

Papa pointed to the dripping child and explained, "Your son here started out to look at the pigs and on the way spotted a young polecat. He tried to catch it! Its mother made sure he didn't!"

"Did he start a fire, too?" Manda asked, looking past the house.

"No, Michael's out back burning Padrac's clothes. And I've scrubbed him down—from head to toe—four times!" answered Papa.

Mama wrapped a light blanket around the boy and tried to soothe him. When she knelt down, Padrac put his arms around her neck and whimpered against her shoulder. Holding him close was almost more than she could stand. She fanned the air in front of her nose, saying, "I'm glad there's a breeze today."

Manda covered her face with her hands and mumbled through her fingers, "I told you he could be a stinker!"

When the excitement and the scent of the skunk died down, Papa remembered to tell Mama, "I saw Sam in town today. I invited him for supper. He said he'd come—said he'd never turn down one of your meals if he could help it!"

Mama smiled at the compliment and said, "Michael went hunting early this morning. We'll be having squirrel stew. Manda, peel a few more potatoes to stretch it. Then there'll be plenty."

"I hope so!" Papa laughed. "You know Sam. He always brings a big appetite."

"Papa, how long have you two been friends?" Manda asked.

"Well, let's see," he said, with a sparkle beginning to show in his eyes. "I first met him back in Tennessee about ten years ago. Then, in December of '32, he came to Texas and we followed after that."

"Oh, I'm so glad he's coming," Manda cried happily. "He always tells such good stories. I especially like the ones about the time he lived with the Indians."

"Manda, he can't tell you his tales tonight," Papa said, and his face became serious. "We have important matters to discuss." The subject was settled and Papa walked out the door.

Manda wanted to insist one little story wouldn't take much time, but she knew better than to argue with her father. She set her mouth in a hard straight line and looked down at the bowl of potatoes in her lap. She finished peeling them in no time. She wondered why she could always do chores faster when she got mad.

Manda set the bowl on the table and said, "Mama, I'm going out to check on the baby pigs. I'm worried about the runt. He isn't growing like the others."

"Listen to me," Mama said kindly. "Don't get attached to that piglet. He's too small to fight for his share. Your father had planned to kill him today so he wouldn't starve to death. But I guess he didn't get to it after all the trouble with Padrac."

Manda bolted out the door yelling, "No! No! I won't let Papa kill him. I'll take care of him. I'll do it!"

Manda took the runt out of the pig pen and held him. He hardly moved in her arms. *Mama's right,* she thought. *He is starving!* Manda knew she must think of a way to save him, and she didn't have much time.

She heard her mother calling, "Manda, come in the house. It's time to set the table."

Gently laying the piglet near its mother, Manda told him, "I'll be back. Don't worry. I won't let them hurt you."

The sound of a horse's hoofs told her their guest had arrived. She walked around the side of the house and saw the tall, well-built man swing down from his horse and shake hands with her father. As always, Manda was happy to see Sam Houston.

Papa had been right. That night, Manda did not get to hear about the time Mr. Houston fought the Creek Indians at Horseshoe Bend with Andrew Jackson, or about how the Cherokee Indians adopted him into their tribe and called him "the Raven."

At first, the men talked of old times in Tennessee. Then Sam Houston asked, "James, is Texas all you thought it would be?"

"Well, I'm not rich yet," Papa replied. "But we had a good crop this year, and we're not wanting for anything."

"There's opportunity here, James," Mr. Houston said. "You should try your hand in the land business."

Papa laughed and said, "No, I'm more suited to farming, Sam. Nacogdoches is growing. There's already a market for cotton."

Mr. Houston nodded. "We just need to settle this thing with the Mexican government."

"We must, Sam! Everybody I talk to agrees! First thing you know, they'll send troops here to take our guns." Papa's voice grew louder, and he banged his fist

on the table. "My grandpappy fought for freedom and I can too. I say we have a right to be free!"

"That's the way, Papa!" Michael said, joining the conversation. "We should have a say in what goes on! Why, they even tell us which church we should belong to."

Manda couldn't understand why her sixteen-year-old brother seemed so anxious for a fight. The talk of war continued throughout supper. Manda tried to eat, but had lost her appetite.

She watched Padrac. He played with his food, unnoticed by either parent. She started to tell on him, but decided he was more entertaining than the talk. On his plate, Padrac made a fence of green beans to pen up a chunk of squirrel. The squirrel kept trying to get out. It finally jumped the fence and landed on the floor. Manda giggled, but no one else paid any attention.

She wished the meal would end so she could go check on the little pig. Manda turned her cup around and around on the table. Staring at the white foam on top of the fresh milk, she made up her mind what to do. She knew it would work!

At last, everyone left the table. By then it was dark, but the two men and Michael went outside.

"Where are they going?" Manda asked.

"Out under the trees," Mama answered. "There they can say things they think we shouldn't hear."

"What things, Mama? Scary things?" Manda wanted to know.

Mama gave her a hug. "Never you mind," she said. "Don't let all this talk upset you."

Manda helped her mother wipe out the dishes. Then she headed for the pig pen. She took a lantern, an old rag, and the cup of milk she had not finished on purpose.

Her idea worked better than she expected. Holding the piglet firmly, she pried open his jaws. She dipped a corner of the cloth in the milk and then forced it into his mouth. To her delight, he sucked on it. Over and

over she fed him, until the piglet would open his mouth before the soaked cloth touched his face. When his stomach grew fat and tight, he fell asleep, and Manda said, "Well, I've started something! I'll need to feed you several times a day, but you'll live. You look so happy and contented now. I know! I'll name you Happy."

Manda's father let her keep the pig, but Happy was strictly her responsibility. Taking care of him, along with her regular chores, kept Manda busy. But they became friends. He went with her everywhere.

The first time Happy followed Manda into the house, her mother threw up her hands and said, "Young lady, I put up with a lot from you and your brothers, but I will not have a pig in my home!"

However, time took care of that. Manda continued to bring Happy inside. She said she couldn't remember to leave him at the door. He was so well behaved, Mama gave up and stopped complaining.

Papa said, "Happy thinks he's a member of the family. Let's not tell him any different."

One hot day in August, Michael walked Manda to the Tanner's farm so she could play with Jane. Mama and Papa wouldn't allow her to walk alone because of the Indians in the area.

Manda told Michael goodbye when she saw Jane waiting under the trees. As she walked toward Jane, she thought she really didn't like her very much, but sometimes Jane did think of fun things to do. And anyway, she was the only girl to play with for miles around.

There was no breeze, and even in the shade of the tall pines the air felt hot and sticky. Neither girl felt like building a pine straw house, so they kicked pine cones as they discussed what to do.

"We can make cornshuck dolls," Manda suggested.

"I don't want to!" Jane replied.

"Then you think of something!" said Manda impatiently.

"I will!" Jane said. "We can go to the creek!"

"Oh, the cool water sounds good," Manda sighed. "But we're not allowed to go by ourselves."

"No one will know," said Jane, becoming excited by the idea. "Mama got some white flour yesterday, and you know how hard it is to come by. So she's busy making bread. She won't miss us."

Manda thought for only a few seconds before she agreed. "All right. Let's go!"

At the creek, the girls took off their shoes and stockings. They let the cool, oozy mud of the shallow edge squeeze between their toes. Holding their skirts high, they slowly waded deeper, until the water covered their knees. With slippery feet, they felt their way, being careful not to step off into a low place.

"Manda, there's no telling what's in this water. Do you feel anything?" asked Jane.

"I feel small fish against my legs every now and

then. But they swim off in a hurry," Manda replied. "Why?"

"Well, I've heard about some dangerous snakes in this creek. If they bite you, you'll die in five minutes," said Jane.

"Really? I haven't heard that. Wouldn't they be afraid of us and swim away?" Manda asked, looking around.

"No, this kind is vicious and not scared of people. And I've heard they're more apt to bite someone with blond hair and fair skin," Jane said almost in a whisper.

"Oh, Jane!" Manda cried. "I have blond hair and fair skin! Let's get out!"

"Manda! Look behind you! I see one swimming toward you now!" shouted Jane.

"Where? I don't see anything. Yes, I do! I see it! I'm getting out," cried Manda. With tears beginning to stream down her cheeks, she struggled to get to the bank.

CHAPTER 3

TALK OF WAR

Just as Manda reached the edge of the water, Jane bent over with laughter. "I was teasing you. You're a baby," she called. Jane laughed so hard, she almost fell down. "It's only a stick floating along! It can't hurt you."

Manda felt her face get hot. She wanted to say something to hurt Jane back, but she was trying so hard not to cry she couldn't talk. She picked up her shoes, with the stockings tucked inside, and started running toward the Tanner's farmhouse.

Jane called after her, "Don't get mad. It was just a joke. You won't tell my mother, will you? If you do, I won't ever play with you again."

Manda didn't answer, but she knew she wouldn't tell anyone. She didn't want to be punished for slipping off to the creek, and she was embarrassed. She would hate for anyone to know how Jane had tricked her. But she wondered *why* Jane had wanted to scare her. Was she really a baby as Jane said?

The girls spent the rest of the afternoon under the pine trees, hardly speaking to each other. Mrs. Tanner thought the day must be too hot for playing.

Manda didn't see Jane again until October when Mrs. Tanner started school. Jane was so glad to have somebody around besides Jeffrey that she behaved. Manda didn't mention the mean trick Jane had played on her, but she had no desire to go wading in LaNana Creek again.

Michael walked Manda to school and back. Sometimes he had to help with the work on their farm, but most days he stayed for the lessons too. Manda knew her father believed in education, and he worked hard to pay Mrs. Tanner to teach his children. She was glad he thought girls as well as boys should attend school.

Walking with her brother through the woods, Manda daydreamed. She especially enjoyed the times Michael walked ahead of her and she could stroll along by herself.

She imagined that the sun reached down through the giant pines with golden fingers to tickle a squirrel, causing it to scamper silently over the pine needles covering the forest floor.

If the animal stopped to look at her, Manda might say, "Good morning, Mrs. Bushytail. How are your babies?"

Manda thought Mrs. Bushytail would answer, "They are almost grown."

When she wore her new blue cape, Manda pretended to be a princess looking over her vast kingdom. She walked under trees whose high arms seemed to reach for the heavens.

Other times she played she was an Indian squaw moving with silent footsteps. Her eyes scanned the woods for a deer to kill for her starving family. Maybe her arrow would find only an unlucky squirrel or rabbit for her children's meal.

One afternoon, Dr. Tanner came in and startled the class when he said, "There's been a battle at Gonzales, but the Texans made short work of it!"

Mrs. Tanner looked frightened. "What happened?" she asked.

"The Mexican commander in San Antonio sent soldiers to take a cannon from the settlers there. They had it for protection against the Indians and refused to give it up. The Texans opened fire, and the Mexicans fled."

Michael spoke up. "What do you think will happen now, Sir?"

"Well, Michael, Houston has been elected commander of troops here in Nacogdoches, and he has asked for men to fight. I'm not sure," said Dr. Tanner, "but I'm afraid we have a war on our hands!"

When the doctor left the room, Manda raised her hand and asked, "Mrs. Tanner? Would you show us the map with the thirteen colonies?"

"Of course, Manda," Mrs. Tanner said, somewhat puzzled over Manda's sudden interest.

Manda's five classmates, including Michael, glared at her in disbelief. How could she ask a question like that, just as the teacher was about to let them go home?

Mrs. Tanner unfolded a worn map and proceeded to point out the states. Manda did not listen to a word she said. Instead, she located their town of Nacogdoches on the map and then found Mexico City. She wanted to see how close the two places were.

Mexico City looked far away. Manda thought surely Sam Houston and his men could chase the Mexican army out of Texas and keep it out. But would he need her father and brother to help him?

Mrs. Tanner finally dismissed the class. Michael hurried out, grumbling about what Manda had done. He sighed deeply and shook his head in apology and disgust to his friend, Ben Nolan. Ben, also sixteen, shook his head back as if to say he felt sorry for Michael's having to put up with a little sister. Ben and his younger twin brothers walked off in the opposite direction.

As Michael and Manda left the red clay and rock for the trail leading through the woods to home, they heard Jane calling. Turning around, they saw her running to catch up with them. They stopped and waited.

When she reached the edge of the forest, Jane had

29

to rest to get her breath before she could talk. "Father sent me to catch you," she said, still breathing hard. "He said he meant to warn you. But you left in such a rush."

Manda stood with her hands on her hips and rolled her eyes upward, waiting to hear what Jane's story would be this time. She remembered the day at LaNana Creek, and she wasn't about to be fooled again.

"Warn us of what?" Michael asked.

"The mad dog," Jane said. "Father said to tell you he saw a sick dog this morning on his way to town. It was foaming at the mouth and acting strange. It ran off behind the trees before he could get a shot at it. He said to be on the lookout for it, and to tell your father."

"All right, Jane. Thanks for telling us. I have my gun and we won't take any chances if we see it," said Michael.

When Jane left, Manda laughed and told Michael, "I'll bet that's another one of her tales. Once she told me a snake was after me. She was lying, but it really scared me. I have the feeling she's making up this story about the mad dog, too."

Michael looked surprised and said, "I don't know Jane as well as you do, but she might be telling the truth. We'll be careful just in case."

On the way home, Michael and Manda didn't see anything unusual, and they both soon forgot about the warning.

As always, Happy was glad to see Manda when she returned home. Manda had to put him in the pen whenever she left to keep him from following her. She fed all the pigs, one of her daily chores, making sure Happy got all he wanted. She told him she would see him later.

Inside the house, Manda poured water from a large pitcher painted all over with pink roses into a matching washbowl. As she washed her hands, she said, "What smells so good?"

Padrac answered her. "Papa shot a rabbit. We gonna eat him with sum dumpers!"

"We're having rabbit and what?" laughed Manda.

"Dumpers," he said. "You know, Manny, dose fat tangs Mama makes like dis," and he patted his hands together.

"Dumplings, Patrick, Dump*lings!*" his mother said.

Manda ran her hand through his curly blond hair and said, "That's all right, Padrac. I knew what you meant."

After supper, Mama and Manda put away the dishes and cleaned the black iron pot they used for cooking in the fireplace. Papa and Michael sat at the table drinking coffee and talking.

"Houston is asking for men to fight," Papa said.

"I hear he leaves tomorrow for San Felipe," said Michael.

"That's right. He's representing us at a big meeting called the October Convention."

Manda ran out the door so she wouldn't hear any more. She sat down on the edge of the porch with her feet on a split-log step. Happy lay beside her, and she rubbed his back. She said to him, "I think I'll just move in with you. You don't scare me with stories of war like they do."

She watched the sun disappear and thought it looked like a giant eye closing behind the trees. Only a dim light was left, and she felt a chill in the air. It told her winter couldn't be far away.

"Manda, time for bed," Mama called.

Manda put Happy in the pig pen and went in the house. Her parents told her good night and went wearily to their room. The boys had already climbed to the loft. Everyone went to bed early on the farm. Manda knew the sun would open his eye all too soon and flood the land with light. Another day's work would be waiting.

When she blew out the lantern on the table, Manda thought the darkness seemed blacker than usual. Only a faint glow remained with the dying logs in the fireplace. Manda fumbled for a piece of kindling wood and touched it to a hot coal. She relit the oil lamp. Then she got down on all fours and looked under her bed. She saw nothing but a few feathers that had fallen out of the mattress. Manda wished she had Happy to keep her company, but the thought of going outside in the night to get him made her tremble.

Manda put out the lamp again and waited for her eyes to adjust to the dark room. She still had the feeling something was under her bed. She was sure if she sat down on the mattress *it* would reach out and grab her feet.

So she got a running start and leaped onto the bed. She pulled the covers up to her chin and snuggled down into the softness of the feather mattress. She lay there remembering when she had lived in Tennessee. Times then were happy. Her family had been full of hopes and dreams—Texas was just a name—and she was never afraid of the dark.

When Manda woke the next morning, she sat up in bed and laughed at herself. *How could I have been so silly last night?* she thought, as she saw the dawn peeking through the cracks around the doors.

Mama came in and started poking up the fire. Soon it blazed up and licked at the new log she had added. "Good morning, Manda," Mama said. "You best go feed the stock now. I'll have hot corn cakes and syrup ready soon. Then it's off to school with you!"

Manda put on a light jacket over her nightgown, picked up the egg basket, and walked out into the cool morning. She opened the barn door and led the two horses out to graze in the pasture. As she started back to get the chicken feed, something startled her. Out of the corner of her eye, she had seen something move by the side of the barn. She hesitated, almost turning toward the house, then straightened her shoulders and walked back into the barn.

"At least I'll not let my imagination get the best of me in the daylight," she said out loud to herself. "It was probably a rabbit or a possum, and I scared him."

She put a scoop of the chickens' grain in a tin pail and hurried out to feed them. She called, "Here, chick, chick," and scattered handfuls of corn with a sweeping motion of her arm. When she had finished, she picked up the egg basket and began to gather eggs from the chicken coop. With her back to the barn, Manda heard a low growling sound. She thought of the bears that lived in the nearby woods.

Manda jerked around to see a dog standing stiffly by the side of the barn. It was black all over and very large. Its mouth looked wet. Its eyes were glazed.

The dog growled again. It bared its teeth. Manda wondered for an instant if it was a wolf. Then the truth hit her. Jane had not lied. This was the mad dog!

Manda just stood there. Her fingers dug into the sides of the egg basket. She couldn't think what to do. She thought if she ran, the dog would chase her. It was a long way to the house. She remembered Papa and Michael were out in the cornfield.

The dog moved toward her.

Manda felt dizzy. Her body tingled. Her mouth went dry. Her legs got so weak, she thought she wouldn't be able to move. And then she did something.

CHAPTER 4

THE BLUE NORTHER

Manda screamed! The dog snarled angrily. It crept closer. Its legs wobbled, but it crouched low and kept coming. Without thinking, Manda threw an egg from the basket. It hit the dog in the face. The thick yellow yolk slid down and hung in the hair on its chin. The dog stopped and shook its head. Then it started for her again. Manda backed toward the house and threw another egg—and another—and another.

A shot rang out! Manda saw the dog fall. She turned and looked behind her. Mama stood on the porch with Papa's gun. She still held it up, ready to shoot again if necessary. With eyes wide, Padrac held on to his mother's skirt.

Manda was the center of attention at school that day. The Nolan twins asked her to tell the story over and over, and Mrs. Tanner let her. Even Jeffrey sat down to listen. Jane tried to take credit for having warned Manda about the dog, but everyone ignored her. Michael tilted his chair back on two legs and beamed with pride at his sister's boldness in not running from the mad dog.

One evening in late November, Papa came home from a meeting and told his family, "There's been fighting in San Antonio, and we hear there's likely to be more. The Texans need men, so Joe Nolan and I are going to help them."

"How long will you be gone, Papa?" asked Manda.

Her father rubbed his bearded chin and answered, "I really don't know. If it weren't for all of you, I think I'd join the volunteer group being formed here and stay until we whipped the Mexicans good and proper!"

"Let me go with you," Michael said. "You know I can shoot a gun as well as any man!"

"No, Michael. Your mother needs you here," said Papa.

With a worried look, Mama asked, "But for now, you're only going to help out, aren't you, James? You'll take care and come back soon, won't you?"

Papa touched her hand and said, "Yes, Katie. We plan to leave in the morning, and we should be back by Christmas."

"Michael and I will take care of things around here while you're gone," Manda said, trying to sound brave.

"Padrac help, too," said the little one.

"That's my boy!" Papa said. "I know you will help by being a good boy and staying out of trouble."

Manda stared into the fire, thinking her worst fear had come true. Papa was leaving! And who knew if he would come back?

That night Manda lay in her bed watching the burning logs in the fireplace. She knew she must close her eyes and sleep before the dancing flames died and left darkness in their place. She had not told anyone about her fear of the dark. She had thought it would go away, but instead it was getting worse. Manda dreaded to see spring come, because then there would be no fire to light her entrance into slumber.

Papa had been gone nearly four weeks when the weather turned bitterly cold. A blue norther dropped the temperature to eighteen degrees. Mrs. Tanner dismissed school until after the first of the year. She said it was too cold for her students to walk to her house. Usually, it didn't get that cold until January or February. But this year many things were different.

For days, Michael had looked forward to spending the weekend with a friend of the family named Hiram Taylor. The elderly man's barn had burned to the ground, and he hired Michael to help him rebuild it. Michael could take his pay in goods from the mercantile store Mr. Taylor owned. In this way, Michael hoped to get a Christmas present for his family.

"Mama, are you sure you and the young'uns will be all right here without me for two days?" Michael asked.

Mama smiled at her tall son and said, "Yes, Dear. We'll be just fine."

"I brought in extra wood for the fire, so you won't need to go out for that," Michael told her. "But I don't like taking our only horse and leaving you without one."

"Papa took his horse," Padrac said.

"Yes, Papa has his horse," said Manda, sighing. "Papa's fighting."

"Don't worry, Michael," Mama said. "Now you be on your way. It's about seven miles, and I want you there before dark. I'm glad Mrs. Tanner let you go at noon today."

"We are too!" Michael and Manda said at the same time.

By mid-afternoon, Mama said, "Why don't I make us a cup of hot tea? Your father managed to get it and I've been stingy with it. We might as well enjoy some. We can sit by the fire and talk before we brave the cold to feed the animals and do the milking."

"That sounds good, Mama," Manda said. "I think I'll peep out the door and see what the weather is doing. A little while ago it seemed to be clouding up."

"Peep out the back door, too, Manny," Padrac said.

"Oh, Padrac, it would be the same, front or back," said Mama, laughing. "But, Manda, don't open the door too wide. You'll let out all the heat. I wish we had windows!"

"Mama, it's sleeting!" cried Manda. "Come look, Padrac. I've only seen it sleet once before—last year on Valentine's Day. I remember, because Papa said there might be ice outside, but we had five warm hearts inside."

"I remember that too," Mama said. "Listen! I can hear the sleet now. It must be coming down harder. You two come drink your tea. Doesn't it smell wonderful?"

"It does, Mama. Maybe it wouldn't if we could have it all the time. I wonder," Manda said.

The sleet stopped, but a fine rain continued as they went to the barn to do the work that had to be done. Manda begged to bring Happy in the house, but Mama told her it would be bad for him to come inside and get warm and then go back to the barn.

"And he's not moving in permanently!" she said with a laugh.

After supper, Manda kept a watch on the weather and reported its progress to her mother.

"Mama! Padrac! Come look!" she called excitedly. "It's sticking to the trees. The pines are almost white."

"Well, they surely are!" Mama said, closing the door against the cold wind. "The rain is freezing on the limbs."

"It's so pretty. It looks like a fairyland. Everything's silvery white. Do you think we'll have snow?" asked Manda.

"It doesn't snow very often here in Nacogdoches. But it might," Mama said, as impressed by the sight as her children were.

After coating the trees and causing long icicles to hang from the house and barn, the rain quit. Mama looked out at the dimly lit, white world, and said, "I think I'll go draw an extra bucket of water before it gets completely dark. We'll need it for coffee in the morning before we have to feed and milk again."

"I'll go with you," said Manda.

"No, you wait here and open the door for me when I come back," Mama told her.

Manda closed the door behind her mother and went to stand by the fireplace. She watched Padrac play on the floor with his wooden animals Papa had whittled for him. She held her hands up to the blazing fire and rubbed them together.

"Mama's taking a long time," said Manda. "That old rope must have frozen. Maybe she needs help pulling up the bucket. I'll go see, but Padrac, you stay here where it's warm."

When Manda opened the door, she heard groans coming from the direction of the well. She cried, "Mama, is that you? Is something wrong?"

Mama answered, "Manda, come help me. I fell."

A thin layer of ice covered the red earth. Twice Manda almost slipped as she hurried to her mother. She found her on the icy ground near the well.

"Mama, are you all right?" Manda cried. "Can't you get up? Here, put your arm around my shoulder, and I'll pull you to your feet."

"I don't think I can put any weight on my left leg. It hurts terribly!" Mama said. "But maybe we can make it if I lean on you. It's so cold out here. I'll be fine when I warm myself by the fire."

Somehow they managed to get back to the house. Mama hopped and tried not to cry out from the pain. She sat down on the bed and with Manda's help lifted her leg and lay down. Manda covered her with a warm blanket. Padrac gave her one of his animals to make her feel better.

After about an hour, Mama said, "I'm afraid my leg is broken. It's beginning to swell, and the pain is getting worse."

"I'll go for help, Mama," Manda said. "You can't lie here all night like this. I'll go get Dr. Tanner."

"Manda, you can't! That's a mile away. It's dark now, and freezing cold. I won't let you!" cried Mama.

"We don't have any choice. I'm used to walking to the Tanner farm. I'll bundle up real good. We'll be back before you know it. Try to sleep," Manda told her. "I'll put a big log on the fire so you'll stay warm. And Padrac, you stay quiet! Just watch after Mama."

"Padrac take care of Mama," he said. "And all dees an-mals will help."

Manda wrapped a wool shawl around her head and put on her rabbit coat. Her father had killed the rabbits last winter, and Mama had sewed the skins together. If felt soft and warm.

"Please be careful," Mama warned. "Turn back if there's any sign of trouble. Oh, how I wish Michael were here."

"Just lie still. I'll be back soon," called Manda. She shivered and stepped out alone into the black night.

CHAPTER 5

CHRISTMAS

Manda knew it would take all the courage she had to walk that mile in the dark. As she entered the familiar path leading through the woods, she was thankful the skies had cleared. At least there was a bright moon. It offered just enough light for her to see the narrow trail.

A cold north wind moaned and caused the icy pine boughs to make crackling sounds overhead. No small animals played now on the forest floor. The weather had forced them to hide away in tree trunks or in burrows underground.

Manda felt so alone. She remembered all the nights when the darkness had frightened her. But she had never been afraid like this. She began to hum a tune she had learned from her father. She thought if she could sing, she might overcome some of her fear.

She raised her voice and sang, "Somebody stole my old coon dog—I wish they'd bring him back." The sound startled her, but she didn't stop. "He'd run the big 'uns o'er the fence—And the little 'uns through the cracks."

A stray cloud blocked the moon. It covered Manda in such darkness she had to feel her way. Each time she wandered from the path, the brambles at the edge pushed her back.

Louder than ever, she launched into the chorus. "Farewell, Old Joe Clark—Bye Minnie Brown. Farewell, Old Joe Clark—Gonna leave this town."

At last, the cloud drifted on its way, and she could see again. She began a new verse. "I used to have an old gray hoss—His name was Henry Dawn. Every tooth in that hoss' head—Could mash a barrel of corn."

Suddenly, Manda knew she was in trouble. Up ahead, and slightly to the right of the path, she saw a pair of eyes shining in the moonlight. She could tell they belonged to a large animal. Then more eyes appeared.

There must be four or five, she thought. *A wolf pack!*

Manda had a decision to make. She could turn and run for home. Or, she could continue on and hope the gnawing in their bellies wouldn't give the wolves courage to attack.

Manda kept walking. "Farewell, Old Joe Clark—Bye Minnie Brown. Farewell, Old Joe Clark—Gonna leave this town," she sang.

Soon she was almost even with the pack. Still they didn't move. She sang out, "When you see that gal of mine—Tell her if you please—When you go to make that bread—Roll them dirty sleeves."

Manda looked straight ahead. She started past the wolves. She could feel their presence. She walked faster. Out of the corner of her eye, she saw their black forms. The wolves began to move around.

"Farewell, Old Joe Clark—Bye Minnie Brown. Farewell, Old Joe Clark—Gonna leave this town," she sang at the top of her lungs.

They were behind her now. She dared not turn around to see if they followed. *Don't run,* she told herself. *Keep singing!* "Raccoon has a bushy tail— Possum's tail is bare—Rabbit has no tail at all—'Cept a bunch of hair."

One of the wolves had begun to howl. A low, mournful wail joined the sound of Manda's voice. The eerie call was almost more than Manda could stand.

Her voice shook as she sang, "Farewell, Old Joe Clark—Bye Minnie Brown. Farewell, Old Joe Clark— Gonna leave this town."

Just as she heard the other wolves join in the howling, she stepped out of the woods into the rocky clearing. With a sigh of relief, she saw the lights from the Tanner farmhouse. The door opened and Dr. Tanner stepped out on the porch. He had heard her singing!

Safe inside the farmhouse, Manda explained why she had come. At once, Dr. Tanner left for the barn to saddle his horse and get ready to leave. Mrs. Tanner wrapped a blanket around Manda and gave her a cup of hot coffee "to warm her innards."

When Manda stopped trembling so much, she told them about the wolves.

Jane laughed and said, "Wolves? Don't you know the wind when you hear it? You really must be a sissy!"

"Shame on you, Jane," Mrs. Tanner said quickly. "And after Manda has come all this way—"

"Didn't you hear them? I *saw* them," Manda said.

Jane just grinned.

Dr. Tanner put Manda on his horse and they started back.

"You're a mighty brave girl," he said. "You have real Texas courage."

Manda smiled. She did not feel brave. Inside, she was still shaking.

Dr. Tanner put a splint on Mama's leg, and told her, "It's not a bad break, but you'll have to stay off it for a while." Winking at Manda, he added, "But I know you'll have plenty of help with your chores."

Manda had just poured the doctor a steaming cup of coffee when she exclaimed, "I hear a horse. Someone's coming!"

Dr. Tanner opened the door and said, "Come see, Manda—and you, too, Padrac."

Manda and Padrac looked out and both cried, "It's Papa!"

They welcomed him home, and everyone tried to

talk at once. Mama told how she had let Michael go away for the weekend, and how Manda had gone for help all by herself.

Padrac said proudly that he had taken care of Mama.

Manda told about the wolves and how scared she had been.

"James, you haven't had a chance to tell us what went on in San Antonio. Was there much fighting?" asked Dr. Tanner.

"Yes—for five days," James told them. "But we ran General Cós out. His army is headed back across the Rio Grande."

The doctor thought a minute and then asked, "What do you think General Santa Anna will do about having one of his generals chased off?"

"I think he'll come after us! We had better get ready!" James said seriously.

Christmas was a joyous time for the Barkers. Manda felt such happiness on Christmas Eve she said, "We just have to do something special to celebrate having Papa back."

"What we gonna' do, Manny?" Padrac asked.

Papa joined in. "I'm game! What do you have in mind, Manda?"

"Well," she said excitedly, "Mr. Stearne told me that when he was a boy back in Germany, people brought trees in the house at Christmas. He said they decorated them with all kinds of things. It's a custom there."

"Imagine! A tree in the house!" Mama said.

So Michael, Manda, and Padrac went into the woods. After inspecting nearly every tree, they decided on a four-foot cedar. Michael made a stand of crossed boards and stood the tree in a corner of the main room.

"What are you going to tie on it, Manda?" Papa asked.

"Mr. Sterne said they used fancy cookies in Germany, so Mama said I could make some, and I'll stick holly with bright red berries in the branches," she answered.

Mama let Manda finish the tree by tying on six silver spoons brought from Tennessee. As they dangled from the green foliage, they reflected the light from the flickering fire.

"Now, if that isn't something to behold!" said Papa, standing back to inspect the strange sight.

The children hung their stockings by the fireplace, with Michael protesting he was too old for such a childish habit. But he was glad the next morning when they found shiny red apples in the stockings. He then surprised everyone with his gift of hard candy from Mr. Taylor's store.

With Mama unable to stand, the rest of the family pitched in. Michael killed a wild turkey, and Papa and Manda put together a fine Christmas dinner. Padrac did his part by saying the blessing over the food.

School started again in mid-January. Manda hated
to leave Happy. She had spent any free time she had
running with him outside or talking quietly to him by
the fire. He liked for her to scratch his soft ears while
he fell asleep. Sometimes she'd tease him by pulling
his rubbery nose.

One morning, when Michael and Manda walked from the woods into the clearing that led to the Tanner home, they saw Jane waiting for them. They knew something must be wrong, as she was always the last one ready for lessons.

With a frightened look on her face, Jane cried, "Hurry! Mama told me to tell you to run to the barn and hide. The Mexican army is headed for Nacogdoches. They're coming to kill us! Mama is waiting to warn the other children. Then we'll hide, too."

"Slow down, Jane. Are you sure? Where is your father?" Michael asked.

"He went to round up men to fight. You had better do what Mama said," cried Jane.

Manda looked at her with doubt and asked, "Who told you the Mexicans were coming this way? We haven't heard anything like that."

Jane glared at Manda and answered, "Well, you don't know everything, Manda Barker! The news just came. A man rode over to tell us."

Remembering Jane had told the truth about the mad dog, Manda grabbed her brother's arm and said, "Come on! Let's go to the barn like she said. I'm scared!"

CHAPTER 6

JANE'S PRANK

As Manda and Michael hurried away, Jane called, "Mama said to cover yourselves with hay, so the soldiers can't see you."

Still thinking it odd Mrs. Tanner did not warn them herself, Michael decided it was best not to take a chance. He covered Manda with the sweet-smelling straw. Then he hid behind some bundles of hay near the barn door. He had his rifle. He planned to fight, if necessary, or to stand guard until help came.

Manda lay on the cold ground, trying to keep from shivering. Soon she heard footsteps running into the barn. Someone started moving the hay around her. With one eye, she peeked through the straw. She saw the twins, Jody and Jamey Nolan, with tears streaming down their cheeks. They were trying to get under the straw.

"I'll help you," said Michael, coming out of hiding.

"You scared me!" Jamey said. "We didn't know anyone else was here."

"We're glad you are, though. We don't want to be alone when they come to shoot us," said Jody.

"Where's your big brother Ben?" Michael asked.

Jody answered. "He had to help Pa today. He walked us over, but went back when we could see the house."

Michael covered up the twins and then waited at his post by the door. He expected Dr. Tanner to return before long.

Inside the house, Mrs. Tanner paced back and forth. She said to Jeffrey, "I wonder why none of the children have shown up for school. I hope nothing has happened. Times are so uncertain!"

She went to the door and called, "Jane, hasn't anyone come yet?"

"No, Mama," came the reply. "But I'm still watching for them. You told us yesterday we had a hard lesson today. Didn't you say we had to know our 'times' or else?"

"Yes, I did. But that shouldn't scare them away. I'm getting mighty worried. It's almost eleven o'clock. Where could they be?" Mrs. Tanner exclaimed.

Another hour passed, and in the barn the children's stomachs told them it was noon. Michael felt he must do something. Anything would be better than waiting, not knowing what was taking place. He could see only one side of the house, but he had not heard any kind of disturbance.

Michael whispered to the others, "Maybe the Mexicans slipped up on the Tanners before they could hide. I'm going to sneak out and see what's going on. Just lie still until I come back."

With caution, Michael slipped out the barn door. Everything seemed normal. Cows grazed peacefully in the fields. He made his way to take a quick look through the one small window. As he raised up from a crouching position, he heard voices.

"When your father gets back, I think he should ride over to the Barkers and find out what's wrong. Then he will probably want to check on the Nolans, too," Mrs. Tanner was saying.

Michael saw Jane sitting at the table eating a helping of venison stew. Her red hair was neatly combed into the two long braids that hung down her back. Each braid was tied at the end with a blue ribbon. She said, "I bet they just didn't want to come to school. When do you think Father will be back?"

"Later this afternoon. He went to check on some sick patients, you know," said Mrs. Tanner.

"Check on patients?" Michael yelled, as he jerked open the door. "Jane told us he went to round up men to fight the Mexicans. She said soldiers were marching on Nacogdoches."

Mrs. Tanner looked at Jane in horror. Jane began to stammer, not knowing how to get out of her lie.

Michael started to go and rescue the others in the barn, but suddenly turned to Jane and accusingly

said, "Jane, it would serve you right if the Mexicans
did come after you. Only, even they wouldn't want
you!"

Mrs. Tanner followed Michael to the barn and
helped brush the hay from the frightened children's

clothes. Sending them on their way home, she went to deal with Jane.

The memory of that day in the Tanner's barn haunted Manda wherever she went. Jane's prank made her realize the army from Mexico really might march across Texas. The grownups talked of nothing but war and fighting. Manda's fear of the dark grew worse.

One night Mr. Nolan came to their house to talk with her father. Manda lay in her bed, trying to go to sleep before her parents put out the lamp. She knew from the look on Mr. Nolan's face he had come with bad news. Manda covered her ears with both hands, but she could hear the men and her mother talking in spite of her effort not to listen.

Joe Nolan said, "Houston sent a letter to Governor Smith saying he wants to resign as commander in chief. He says his job is impossible with everyone disagreeing over how to fight the Mexicans. So the governor gave him leave and he's gone to try and make a peace treaty with the Cherokees. He wants their promise that they won't cause trouble too."

"I hate to hear that. We need Sam, but I can see why he feels as he does. His hands have been tied. The men at the Alamo refuse to obey his orders. By the way, how are things there? Have you heard anything new?" Manda's father asked.

"Only that William Travis and twenty-five men

have joined the others defending the Alamo. And David Crockett came through town today, going to give them a hand. Crockett's picking up men along the way. I hear that two from Nacogdoches went with him," Joe said.

"Fannin has stayed in Goliad," Papa said, "because he thinks we should make a charge against the enemy first, and not wait for Santa Anna to come find us."

"Well, who knows what would be best? Maybe you and I ought to go find a fight somewhere," Joe said.

"I feel the same way," Papa agreed, "but the last time I left home, my family suffered. Katie broke her leg, and it could have been worse. We don't know what the Indians around here might do with the Mexicans stirring them up. If we Texans just knew what we were doing..."

"True, true!" Joe said, closing the door.

Michael had listened to the men's conversation. When the door shut, he said, "So David Crockett came to Nacogdoches today, and I didn't get to see him! Do you think he had his gun Betsy with him?"

"I'm sure he did, Son. You heard about the time he aimed his Betsy at a raccoon in a tree, and the animal said, 'Is that you, Davy? I know when I'm a gone coon! Don't shoot. I'll come on down.' He recognized Crockett and just gave himself up!"

Manda drifted off to sleep. She slept restlessly until about three o'clock, when she woke screaming.

"No! No! Get out!" she cried.

CHAPTER 7

THE RUNAWAY SCRAPE

Papa went to Manda's bed to comfort her. He shook her gently and said, "Manda, Manda, wake up! You're having a bad dream."

"Oh, Papa," she sobbed. "The Mexicans were coming in our door. Mr. Houston stood by the fireplace, but he didn't try to help. Three tall soldiers with swords came to kill us. You weren't here—just Mama, the boys, and me."

"Hush, now. I am here, and you're safe. You've heard too much war talk. I'll sit on the side of your bed until you fall asleep again," Papa said. "Try not to think about it."

"I'll try," said Manda. "Will you tell me a story? That would help."

"All right, but just one. What do you want to hear?" Papa asked.

"Tell me about Uncle Fred and the bear," she said.

"Well, when I was a boy, back in Tennessee, my father told this tale on Fred, his older brother. Uncle

Fred went bear hunting one day in a thick wooded area not far from his home. He spotted a big black bear at some distance and aimed his rifle. He fired and missed. The noise made the bear mad, and it started toward Uncle Fred. Fred was so scared, he dropped his gun and began to run. The two of them ran through the woods, dodging trees and jumping over logs.

"The bear was gaining on him. Fred came to a huge

oak tree and thought about climbing it. But he knew the bear would follow him up the tree and trap him there. So he pulled his knife from his belt and thought he at least would fight back when the bear caught him.

"Uncle Fred ran around the tree, and the bear ran after him. He knew if he stopped, the bear would have him, so he kept running. Around and around they went, with Fred holding the knife high in the air. The bear must have gotten tired or bored with the chase. It suddenly stopped!

"Fred didn't expect that. He was still running, and ran right into the critter. When he hit it, Fred fell onto the bear's back, and his arm came down. He got the bear square in the neck with his knife. The bear fell over dead. Uncle Fred said he planned it that way, but he never did go bear hunting again."

Manda smiled sleepily and closed her eyes.

By the first of March, the men of Nacogdoches had trouble staying with their plows long enough to get the ground ready for spring planting. To find out the news from San Antonio, they met in town—in the old stone fort, or in groups on the street. The war was all they had on their minds.

When word from the Alamo reached Nacogdoches, Papa rushed home to tell his family.

"All the Texans were killed," Manda heard her father say, as he came in the door.

"Where, Papa?" she asked.

"At the Alamo in San Antonio," he answered. "They put up a good fight, but they were outnumbered. They didn't have enough men to stand up against so many Mexican soldiers."

"Didn't any more men go to help?" Michael asked.

"Only a few," Papa said. "Colonel Fannin started out from Goliad, but had trouble and turned back."

"Papa, if they knew they were outnumbered, why didn't they try to escape?" asked Manda.

"They thought it best to fight the Mexicans there and give Houston time to raise an army. Santa Anna sent word he would take no prisoners but instead would kill them all. A cannon shot was the Texans' answer," Papa told them.

Mama said sadly, "Then they stayed, knowing they all would die."

"Yes," Papa said. "It was told that when Travis learned help was not coming and all hope seemed lost, he drew a line in the dirt with his sword. He stepped across the line and asked who would join him in staying to fight. They were free to leave if they wanted to. Men began crossing the line. Jim Bowie was so sick he couldn't get off his cot, but asked to be carried across. Every man but one chose to fight until death."

Seeing the scene in her mind, Manda asked, "How do you know all this, if everyone was killed?"

"All the fighting men were killed, Manda," Papa

said. "But there were women and children in the fort, too. Santa Anna sent a soldier's widow to tell the Texans what happened."

It seemed to Manda that every time her father went into town, he came back with sad news. Toward the end of March, he told of more bloodshed. James Fannin and his men had left Goliad to join forces with General Houston. Near Coleto Creek they were attacked by the Mexican army. The Texans surrendered on the promise they would be prisoners treated with honor. Instead, on orders from General Santa Anna, they were marched out on the prairie and shot.

More important to Manda was her father's other announcement.

Papa gathered his family around him and said, "I'm leaving tonight to join Houston's army. Charles Tanner, Joe Nolan, and most of the men in Nacogdoches are going."

"No, Papa! You can't go! We need you here," Manda cried.

"Texas needs me more," he told her. "The time has come—either we fight to make Texas free, or lose everything we've worked for! Santa Anna won't stop. He plans to drive all Americans out of Texas."

"I'm going with you, Papa. You can't say no. Texas needs me too!" said Michael.

"All right, Michael. I can't refuse you this time," Papa said. "Some younger than you are going, I suspect. Texas is your home too. You have a right to fight for her."

Padrac had listened, but he didn't understand. He said, "Papa, me and Manny want to go. We like goin' places."

"No, Padrac," Mama answered. "You and Manda will stay here with me. I'll need your help to keep the farm going."

Manda took Padrac by the hand and went out on the porch. Her body shook with anger. "I won't even tell him goodbye," she said. "Papa could stay here if he wanted to. No one is making him join that old army. How much difference can one more man make?—well, two men, with Michael going too."

She watched Padrac chase the chickens in the yard and said to Happy, who lay beside her, "I wish I'd never heard of that old war!"

Manda did tell her father and brother goodbye. But she was still mad as she watched them ride off together on Papa's horse. They planned to stop at Hiram Taylor's place to pick up more horses Mr. Taylor wanted to send to General Houston. Since he was old and in bad health, Mr. Taylor couldn't go with the other men.

That night, Manda heard sobs coming from her mother's room. It seemed as though the approaching Mexican army cast a black shadow over Texas, covering all of it in darkness. Manda hated being afraid.

She didn't know if she would ever see Papa or Michael again. At last, she cried herself to sleep.

Padrac slept in the loft alone. He was too young to understand that the happy life he knew might soon just be a memory.

Mrs. Tanner stopped holding classes. With most of the men gone, the women and children stayed close to home. They kept the doors bolted and a gun loaded.

One morning, the patter of rain woke Manda before daylight. She lay in the dark room wondering where Papa and Michael had slept that night. She pulled the covers over her head and said a quick prayer. She asked for protection for her father and brother and ended with, "Please don't let anything get me, and hurry and make the sun come up. Amen."

Manda heard a door open, and then footsteps. She lay still and listened. Whoever was in the room walked quietly. *An Indian!* Manda thought. *I won't move and maybe he won't notice me.* The footsteps came closer, and closer...

"Manda, take that quilt off your head! You'll smother! I know you're awake," Mama said, as she opened the front door and looked out.

Manda jerked off the covers and sat up. "Oh, Mama, it's you," she said. "Look at that rain! Is it ever going to stop?"

"Surely it will soon," Mama replied. "It has rained for eight days straight. I'm glad we live a piece away from both creeks. They're probably over their banks by now."

Padrac heard them talking and climbed sleepily down from the loft. He said, "I'm hungry!"

"Well, you come go with Manda and me to do the milking and gather the eggs. Then I'll make you a nice breakfast," Mama said. She picked up the loaded rifle, and they went together to do chores.

They ate their morning meal without talking. The dreary, rainy day caused each one to miss the men of the family in their own special way. The sound of a horse's hoofs broke the silence.

"Miz Barker! Miz Barker!" a voice called urgently.

Mama ran to the door and saw old Hiram Taylor sitting on his horse. He seemed in a hurry to be on his way.

He yelled out, "Run, Miz Barker! Some men rode into town and said the Mexicans and Indians have banded together. They're camped about thirty miles south of here and headed this way. The Safety Committee says to leave. Fly! Fly for your lives!"

Before Mama could ask any questions, he rode off to warn more families. His horse's hoofs made holes in the soaked ground.

For an instant, Mama stared after Mr. Taylor. Then, without a word, she ran from the door to the barn. She led the horse out and began to hitch him to the small

wagon. Her voice shook when she shouted, "Manda! Patrick! Bring the rest of those corn pones and grab anything else we can eat. Gather up some quilts, and Manda, get the gun! And hurry!"

CHAPTER 8

ON THE ROAD

Manda's heart pounded as she and Padrac carried the food and other things to their mother. Manda thought of her dream. Would the Mexicans get to their house before they could get away?

The stress in his mother's voice scared Padrac. He began to cry. "Where we goin'? I dint get frue eatin'," he said.

"Just get in the wagon, Patrick! There's not much time," Mama said. "We have to get out of Texas!"

Manda looked into Mama's eyes and asked, "Are you afraid too?"

"Manda, it's time to be afraid," Mama told her. "Leaving like this is the only thing I know to do. We'll just pray we get to come back."

Manda had never realized her mother could be scared, but it made her feel better to know she wasn't the only one who was frightened.

Manda climbed on the wagon and tried to calm Padrac. All of a sudden she jumped down and ran toward the pig pen screaming, "Happy! I can't leave Happy!"

"Manda, come back!" Mama called. "We can't take that pig!"

Manda returned with Happy trotting beside her. "He won't slow us down, Mama," she said. "He'll run along behind us. Happy has a lot of energy."

Mama climbed up and took the reins. She hesitated, then shoved them in Manda's hands and cried, "Hold these! I must get something!"

When she ran back to the wagon, Mama carried the family Bible, a piece of soft deerskin, and her six silver spoons engraved with a *B*. "Wrap these and hide them as best you can! Gitty-up!" she yelled.

Manda and Padrac covered themselves with the quilts and huddled together in the back of the wagon. Mama drove the horse hard. She seemed unaware of the rain beating against her face and soaking her clothes.

They took the old North Road that led to town. Mama whipped the horse to make him go faster. Happy had a hard time keeping up until Mama slowed down because of other people crowding the road.

As they turned east onto the Old San Antonio Road, Manda looked around her. Rolling hills circled the town. Manda could see people coming from three directions. They joined together to travel one path east.

"Where are they coming from?" she cried.

"From all around," Mama answered. "Folks from all over Texas are running—the same as we are!"

As they passed the square, Manda saw men, assembled and ready to defend their town. Most were old like Hiram Taylor. He stood among them and waved when he recognized the Barkers. He carried his rifle, ready to do his part in holding back the enemy until the women and children could escape.

"Where are we going?" Manda yelled over the noise of the people.

"We'll take this Old San Antonio Road to the Sabine River. Then we'll cross the river into Louisiana. There, in the United States, we'll be safe," Mama said.

The long line of people traveled at a slow pace. As far as Manda could see, women, children, and old men struggled to flee the Mexican army. Some rode horses or oxen; some rode in wagons. But most of them walked. Some carried possessions grabbed in haste. Others had nothing but the clothes on their backs.

The motion of the wagon had lulled Padrac to sleep. When he woke, he whined, "I'm hungry."

"Manda, give him a piece of corn bread. We may as well eat some, too. We still have a long ride ahead of us," Mama said.

"I brought the crock of hominy," Manda told her. "It will help fill our stomachs."

Manda took several bites. The food tasted good. On the side of the road, a woman with three young children walked. The small boys, with tired and dirty faces, watched Manda eat. Manda knew from the look in their eyes, they were hungry.

"Mama, I'll walk for a while," she said. "I want to tie Happy to the wagon. I'm afraid he'll get lost or someone will steal him. Why don't we let those children ride and catch their breaths?"

"All right, but only if you stay close by where I can keep an eye on you," Mama agreed.

As Manda changed places with the children, she gave them the remaining corn pones and hominy. The woman thanked her and said they hadn't eaten since the morning before.

Manda took care of Happy, and she and the woman walked together. The woman told Manda they had come from west of Nacogdoches, and said, "Thank goodness, the rain has slacked off for a while."

By late afternoon, the boys had rested, and Manda took her place back in the wagon.

All at once, Mama cried, "Manda, I think I see the Tanners up ahead. They're all walking. Jump down and go tell them to wait for us. We can share our wagon."

Manda ran. She longed to see some familiar faces, even Jane's. She passed a woman pushing a hand cart containing four children. Another woman pulled her children on a crude sled that had been made to haul wood. Manda saw panic in the mothers' eyes.

As soon as she got close enough, Manda called out to the Tanners. They waited together until Mama got

there with the wagon. They were overjoyed to see each other, and the two families went on, taking turns riding. Mama's leg hurt her in damp weather, but she insisted on walking as much as she could.

Jane complained constantly. "I'm tired," she whined. "And when are we going to get something to eat?"

By now everyone was hungry and tired. Manda's legs ached, and her shoes began to rub blisters on her feet. Her stomach growled from being empty, and even when it was her turn to ride in the wagon, Manda's body cried out for rest.

"Mama, how much farther do we have to go?" Manda asked. "It will be dark soon."

"We're almost to Attoyac Creek," Mama said. "We'll have to rest tonight and make the crossing early in the morning when we can see better."

"Let's get off the road and look for a high piece of ground where we can sleep," suggested Mrs. Tanner. "I see others doing the same thing. Maybe out of sight we'll be safe."

They chose a spot on the side of a hill. The ground was wet, but not standing in water like other parts. There were trees to hide them if the enemy came. They had nothing to eat, but they were so tired, they slept anyway.

The sound of Jane's voice waked Manda at daybreak. Jane cried excitedly, "I was looking for something to eat, and I met an old man. He is all alone, and he has food! He asked us to join him in a little while for some roasted pork. I said we would."

"Where is he?" Mrs. Tanner asked.

"Just right over there," Jane said, pointing through the trees.

Manda rubbed her eyes and looked around for Happy. She knew he must be hungry, too. When she didn't see him, she reasoned he must be rooting around in the woods for food.

Suddenly, a horrible thought struck her. Jane had said, "roasted pork!"

Manda screamed, "Happy! Happy!" and ran in the direction Jane had pointed.

Then she heard Happy squeal. She ran toward the awful noise and yelled, "Stop! Stop!"

When she got to them, what she saw almost made her heart quit beating. The old man strained to hold on to one of Happy's legs. In his other hand he held a knife. Happy squealed and struggled to get loose.

Manda grabbed the man's arm and cried, "You can't do that! He's mine! He's my pet!"

The man let Happy go. He told Manda a girl with red hair had brought him the pig and had said he could eat some if he would cook it. He was hungry and willing to help her out.

Manda said, "We're hungry, too. But we'll have to find something else to eat."

Manda stormed back to her family with Happy

close behind her. In a loud voice, she told everyone what Jane had done. She was so mad, she started to cry. Mama tried to comfort her while Mrs. Tanner shamed Jane. But in their rush to get back on the road and to Attoyac Creek, the incident seemed quickly forgotten.

"They can make light of it if they want to," Manda told Happy. "But I won't ever forget this!"

When they rejoined the fleeing Texans, Manda thought the road seemed more crowded than ever. She heard the cries of children who were tired and hungry. She saw a woman raise her hands to the sky and wail pitifully, "Help us! All is lost!" Others joined her until the sorrowful moaning caused Manda to cover her ears.

About the middle of the morning, they reached the creek. Because of all the rain, it had overflowed its banks. As they approached the water, Manda saw horses and people swimming across. Many mothers had to make several trips, carrying one child at a time. They left behind everything they had. They now thought only of saving their lives.

To Manda's surprise, Mama yelled, "Hold on!" and drove the horse off the road as far as she could into a thicket.

"I've crossed this Attoyac before when the water's been up. I know a place where it's not so deep. We'll walk up it a ways," she said. "Manda, get the rope."

Mama unhitched the horse, and they quickly threw

limbs and brush around the wagon. She said, "By some chance, if we get to come back, maybe it will be here. It's old and rickety, but better than nothing."

They walked through the soggy bottom toward the place where the creek became more shallow. Manda slapped at the insects flying around her head and kept a watchful eye out for snakes. Padrac lost a shoe in the mud and pitched the other one into the rushing water before his mother could stop him.

Manda and Jane had nothing to say to each other. Manda made sure Happy stayed away from Jane, but that was easy because Happy ran whenever Jane moved in his direction. He seemed to know what Jane had tried to do. He rolled over and over on the slushy ground. The cool mud must have felt good on his dry skin.

"This is it," Mama said. "There's still a strong current here but it's not as deep. And we're better off away from those panic-stricken people. If we're to survive, we must stay calm."

Mrs. Tanner tied one end of the rope to a tree. Then Mama waded into the water to cross the creek. Manda held her breath as she watched her mother leave them. What if Mama's leg suddenly gave out? No one was there to help her if she ran into trouble.

When Mama reached the rushing water in the middle, Manda could see she was having a hard time. Mama struggled against the current to keep from being swept downstream.

Manda had a sick feeling in her stomach. "Please, God, let her get to the other side," she prayed.

It was not until Manda heard her mother call, "I made it!" that she realized she had closed her eyes, afraid of what she might see.

"Thank you, God," she whispered.

Mama tied the other end of the rope to a tree on the opposite side of the creek. She came back and took Padrac and the horse across. Holding on to the rope, the Tanner children followed. Mama yelled to Manda to hurry.

"Goodbye, Happy," Manda said, trying not to cry. She patted her pig one last time. "You wouldn't make it if I took you with me. You'll be safer here in the woods. I'll look for you if we get to come back."

Happy cocked his head to one side and looked at Manda as if he didn't understand why she was leaving him. He started to follow her, but stopped when she told him to go back.

With tears in her eyes and one hand on the rope, Manda waved to him and made her way into the water. Mrs. Tanner crossed last when Manda was safe on the other side.

In time, the Barkers and Tanners again joined the hundreds of families traveling east on the Old San Antonio Road. Mama had managed to take the rifle and the Bible in which she had recorded the births of her children. She rode the horse, because her leg was becoming quite painful. Manda, Padrac, and the Tanners trudged along beside her.

The six of them hardly talked, they were so weak from hunger. When they saw a farmhouse, a good distance from the road, Mrs. Tanner suggested they take time to go ask for something to eat.

"We're going to fall in our tracks if we don't get some food soon," she said.

They reached the house only to find it empty. The door stood open. They went in and found freshly baked bread and eight hen's eggs, which Mama cooked over the still-hot coals in the fireplace. The home looked as if it had been left in a hurry. Manda's mother said she knew the owners wouldn't mind if hungry families helped themselves.

After feeding the horse from a heaping corn crib and resting a bit, Mama said, "Hurry, everybody! We'd best get started."

Mama insisted Mrs. Tanner ride for a while and hold Jeffrey in front of her on the horse. She said her leg felt better. But Manda saw that she limped slightly when she walked. Mrs. Tanner must have noticed it too, for she refused to take the horse.

Just before they got back on the road, Jane screamed and fell to the ground.

"What's wrong, Jane?" Mrs. Tanner asked, running to her daughter.

"It's my ankle," moaned Jane, thrashing about as though in pain.

"Rest a minute," Mrs. Tanner told her. "And then see if you can stand on it."

It was no use. No matter how much they tried to help her, Jane wouldn't put any weight on her foot.

"The poor child," Mama said. "She's sprained it. Here, let's lift her up on the horse. She can ride. I'm sure I'm in better shape than she is, now."

Again, they camped in the woods that night. They each ate only one piece of the bread brought from the farmhouse, saving the rest for morning. Huddled together under a large oak tree, they fell asleep exhausted.

Hours later, Manda waked up. She saw something moving in the darkness a few yards from them. She just *knew* it was a Mexican soldier. She lay stiff with fright, trying to decide if she should risk making noise to wake her mother.

Then, as she peered harder into the dark, she realized her imagination had played a trick on her. What she had seen was only a half-broken limb hanging from a tree. As it hung there, the wind blew it slowly back and forth.

All of a sudden, Manda felt Jane get up. She saw her run quietly on tiptoe to where the leftover bread had been wrapped in leaves. Jane broke off a chunk and hurried back to her place on the ground to eat it.

Manda wondered—*Could a sprained ankle heal so soon?* She thought not. But she would wait until morning and find out.

CHAPTER 9

VICTORY AT SAN JACINTO

Manda waked up early. She wondered if she had even been asleep. Then she remembered what she had seen during the night, and was anxious to know if Jane would walk that morning.

Manda was not surprised when Jane waked up crying and complaining again. Jane said her ankle felt no better than the day before. Manda watched her and waited. They ate the hard bread and prepared to leave the woods.

Mrs. Tanner and Mama started to lift Jane onto the horse, and Manda could be silent no longer. Shaking, she cried out, "Jane Tanner, this is too much! It's one thing to play mean tricks on me, but I won't let you do it to my mother. You can walk fine. I don't think you hurt your ankle in the first place. Admit it! Tell your mother the truth. Tell her! Tell her you can walk!"

"No, I can't! You hush! You're cruel to say such a thing," Jane yelled, wrinkling her face into an ugly frown.

Manda glared at her and said simply, "I saw you last night—when you got the piece of bread."

"Jane, what is Manda talking about? Tell me the truth!" Mrs. Tanner demanded.

Jane began to cry. Between sobs, she said, "All right, it's true! I can walk. But I am so tired—and so scared."

"Oh, Jane," her mother said. "I'm ashamed of you! You've been thinking only of yourself. We're all scared, but we're trying to be brave."

Mrs. Tanner put her arms around Jane and added, "We're going to be all right, but all of us must do our part. We don't have time or patience for lies and pitching fits."

No one said much after that. They took turns on the horse, but when they walked, it took all their energy. They were wet and cold and blisters burned their feet.

Manda wondered why she saw carts and wagons left by the side of the road. She found out when her mother yelled, "Look out!" and shoved her out of the way. A woman driving a one-horse wagon full of children would have hit them if Mama hadn't seen her coming.

The woman kept trying to pass others on the road. She screamed at her horse and wore a frown on her face. In her desire to get ahead of everyone else, she didn't seem to care whom she hurt. Finally, the wheels of the wagon left the packed surface of the road and bogged down in the mud. The horse couldn't pull them loose. The woman pleaded with the people nearby to help her.

They all walked on as though they hadn't heard her begging. In a while, she gave up. She yelled something ugly and jerked her children out of the wagon, as if getting stuck was their fault. She unhitched the horse and sullenly took her place in the line.

Later, two men on horseback rode by shouting, "The Indians and Mexicans have taken Nacogdoches! They're burning everything!"

Manda thought she would never see her home again. Her feet felt so heavy it was an effort to take each step. But she hung her head and walked on. Manda looked down at her shoes caked all over with red mud. She thought about the Mexican army marching into Texas, and about the people who had started with so much hope now making footprints in the mud to leave. Quiet tears made streaks down her dirty cheeks.

Mama looked at her and said, "Hush now! We don't even know if those men were telling the truth. They looked like army deserters to me. We're safe, and we'll get to the border tomorrow."

Manda knew they had reached the Sabine before she saw the water. The crowd of people, no longer in a line, fanned out right and left along the bank. Tempers were short. Often, Manda heard angry words.

"Why is everyone just standing around?" she asked.

"From what I can see, there's only one ferry to take us across," Mama answered.

Mrs. Tanner said, "I heard a man say the river is so

high, the ferry has to travel over half a mile to cross it. We'll have to wait our turn."

"I hope it won't be long," Jane said.

The news spread through the crowd that only women and children were allowed to board the ferry. They were being carried to a small island in the middle of the river, because it took too much time to go all the way to the Louisiana side. Manda felt sorry for the old men as they left the others to search for a way to cross the swollen waters.

The Barkers and Tanners waited. Each time a group boarded the ferry, those remaining on shore moved closer to their turn and safety.

Rain clouds hovered overhead, bringing dusk early. Mrs. Tanner wondered aloud if the ferry would close down at dark. The longer they waited, the more afraid Manda became of being trapped. She knew if the Mexicans and Indians came, there would be no place to run.

When a rider approached, shouting in a hoarse voice, Manda thought the dreaded attack had begun. The man's horse was covered in foam, showing that he had ridden hard. She grabbed Padrac and held on to her mother's arm. "What is he saying?" she asked.

"I can't hear him," Mama replied. "But look! Women are cheering and throwing their bonnets in the air. It must be good news!"

The man passed closer, and they understood his words. He said, "The Texas army whipped the Mexi-

cans on the plains of San Jacinto! Stop! Go back to your homes!"

Manda, Mama, Padrac, and the Tanners joined in as people began to shout and dance around together. They all laughed and talked. They said prayers of thanks and asked for the safety of their men. Generous farmers on the Louisiana side of the river sent food over on the ferry. As weary as the people were, hardly anyone slept that night.

Two days later, after a rest, the runaways began the long trek home. They were still tired, but happy hearts made the trip bearable.

Manda felt so joyful, she skipped along, ignoring the blisters on her feet. She looked up at Padrac, who was riding with their mother, and teased him saying, "When we get home, I'm going to teach you to speak better. You know, you're the man of the house until Papa and Michael get back."

Padrac had a puzzled look on his face. He said, "Me not a man. Me dis a lil' boy, Manny."

Manda decided to try to get along with Jane. She talked to Jane about things they could do together when they got home. Jane seemed to want to be pals again. She offered Manda some dried beef and biscuits she had in the pocket of her apron.

At the Attoyac Creek, two men had made a raft and were taking women and children across. Manda was glad they didn't have to swim this time.

"Mama, do you think our wagon will still be there?" Manda asked when they got to the other side.

"I hope so! We'll go into the thicket and see," Mama said.

The two families parted and Mrs. Tanner called, "See you at home. We'll celebrate when the men return."

At no time did the two women allow themselves to question that their husbands and son would come back.

"We'll look forward to it. Let us hear from you," Manda's mother said.

As they walked through the woods, Manda kept glancing around, hoping to see Happy. But there was no sign of him. They did find the wagon where they left it, covered with brush. The silver spoons were safely hidden under the wet quilts. Mama hitched up the horse.

This time she drove the wagon slowly out of the thicket. Just before they reached the road again, Manda heard a noise behind them. "Someone's following us," she cried.

"It's probably an animal," Mama told her. "But we're safe here in the wagon."

The sound of something running through the brush came closer.

"It's catching up with us," Manda said. Then she let out a yell. "Mama, it's Happy! Stop! I didn't think I'd ever see him again."

Manda jumped down from the wagon and began to hug the muddy pig. He looked thinner, but Manda thought it was a miracle he was even alive. She talked her mother into letting him ride in the back of the wagon, at least part of the way. The Barkers headed home.

"Look!" Manda cried, as they passed a farm. "The house has been burned to the ground. Nothing's left but the chimney."

They found out there had been no Mexicans or Indians in the town. The riders had lied. But with everyone gone, bad men had ridden through the countryside, robbing the empty houses and burning some.

When their own farm finally came into view, Manda was relieved to see the log house still standing. She said, "That's the sweetest sight I've ever seen!"

Once inside, Mama shook her head, saying, "They've taken everything but the furniture—all our food and clothes—the iron pot and dishes—and I know they cleaned out the smokehouse!"

"Why did somebody steal our things?" asked Manda.

"They'll sell them," Mama told her. "Look, they even emptied the feathers out of the mattresses. They probably used the ticking to carry everything in. At least they left our chickens."

"I don't see my rabbit coat, or Padrac's wooden animals," Manda cried. "Oh, Mama! They took the pitcher and washbowl Grandma gave you when we left Tennessee!"

"Children, come here," Mama said. "We're safe and together. That's what's important. And I know in my heart, your father and brother are all right and will come home soon. Then we'll be a family again, living in a free land. What more could we ask for?"

That night Manda, Padrac, and Mama slept together on the floor. Early the next morning, Manda sat up with a start. What had waked her? She thought she had heard a noise outside the cabin. Everything was quiet now, but she had the feeling something was wrong. She sat still and listened.

She heard it again! Somebody was talking outside. Quietly, Manda got up, opened the front door a crack, and looked out.

Indians!

CHAPTER 10

TOGETHER AGAIN

Manda saw a group of Indians down by the smoke-house. She carefully closed the door and bolted it. Then she ran back to where her mother lay sleeping and shook her saying, "Mama! Mama! Wake up! There are Indians outside!"

Mama sat up quickly and shook her head to clear it. After a few moments, she said calmly, "Wake Padrac while I get the gun. Then you two hide."

Manda did as she was told. Before Padrac knew what was happening, she had him hugged with her in a corner of the room.

"Is dis a new game, Manny?" he asked.

"Hush, Padrac," Manda said. "We mustn't make a sound."

The three of them waited. Mama stood by the door and held the rifle. They heard the Indians talking but couldn't understand their language.

"They don't know we're here," Mama said.

Before long, the Indians walked onto the porch. They rattled the door, but couldn't budge it.

"They may break it down," Mama whispered. "I'm going to see what they want."

She opened the door and raised the gun as she stepped outside. She yelled, "Go away! Get off our property!" There was silence. Then Mama called, "Manda! Padrac! It's all right! They want food. They don't look like they're from around here."

Manda and Padrac walked slowly out on the porch and stood close to their mother. Manda watched the dark-skinned people, four of whom were children. They were dressed in buckskin and calico, and the men had feathers stuck in their black hair. All of them wore leather moccasins on their feet. Manda noticed mud on their clothes and thought they looked tired.

The oldest squaw mumbled and pointed to her mouth. A younger brave held up his hand in a sign of peace.

Mama explained to the Indians as best she could that the meat in the smokehouse had been stolen, but she would feed them. The Indians told her in sign language and broken English they had fled to Louisiana. They were now trying to return to their home in the Big Thicket, south of Nacogdoches.

Mama knew the house would be crowded, so they built a fire outside and roasted chickens on a spit. The Indian women picked young beans and squash from

the garden. They cooked in a clay pot they carried with them. Everyone sat on the ground to eat.

Manda had fun trying to talk to the Indian children. She pointed to herself and to one of the men. Then she pretended to be shooting a gun. A boy nodded his head to show he understood that her father was away fighting.

When they finished eating, the boy untied a leather pouch he wore tied around his waist. He drew a circle in the dirt and emptied some smooth round stones out of the pouch. Tossing and rolling the stones, he showed Manda how to play an Indian game.

The next afternoon, the Barkers had another surprise. Manda and her mother were pulling weeds in the garden; Padrac was picking and eating dewberries nearby. When Manda stretched to rest her back, she said, "Look, Mama. Some men are headed this way."

Mama raised up and saw two riders on horseback at the top of the hill. At first she couldn't tell who they were. As they came closer, she cried, "Can it be?"

The men waved and shouted and spurred their horses to go faster. Manda started running and screaming. "It is! It is! Papa and Michael are home!"

After hugs all around, Papa said to Padrac and Manda, "Let me look at you. I believe you've changed since we've been gone."

"Yes, Padrac, your face is purple!" laughed Michael.

"I dint eat *all* da berries," Padrac insisted, shaking his head.

Mama said, "Patrick, come here so I can wipe off your mouth."

"No, Mama," Padrac said, starting to cry. "If you wipe off my mouf, I can't talk anymore!"

Mama smiled. "Patrick, I meant I would wipe the berry juice off your mouth."

Manda said, "It's good to have our family back to normal again."

"Oh, James, we have so much to talk about," Mama said.

"I know," he said, "but first, are you all alright?"

"We're fine. We had a terrible scare, and everything was taken out of the house, but it's over now. We're together. Come, let's sit under the trees, and you tell us about San Jacinto. We've heard stories, but you and Michael were there," said Mama.

"We were there, sure enough," Michael said, "but we thought we'd never get to fight!"

"Because Houston kept retreating," Papa added.

"We were tired of running, and rarin' for a fight! We thought General Houston had lost his nerve. Then he did it!" said Michael.

Papa explained, "Sam ordered the attack in the middle of the afternoon. He led us across a grassy field, and we surprised Santa Anna's troops. They were resting—some were even asleep. We yelled, 'Remember the Alamo!' and 'Remember Goliad!'"

"And old Santa Anna got away, but our men found him the next day," Michael said with a chuckle.

"Did you see him? What did he look like?" Manda wanted to know.

"Nobody knew who he was until his men started saying *'Presidente, Presidente.'* He had dressed himself in peasant's clothes to try to escape," Michael told her.

The family stayed up late, telling about things that had happened while they were apart and making plans for the future.

Padrac began having trouble keeping his eyes open. When Mama noticed him she said, "It's time for you to go to sleep. You can hear more stories tomorrow."

Padrac looked at her with half-closed eyes and said, "Sleepin's not good for you—dere's nuthin' to do!"

Manda just shook her head.

That night, Manda lay in total darkness, thinking about the events of the past weeks. She stretched and shifted her body. She felt relaxed and at peace. Suddenly, she realized she wasn't afraid of the dark anymore. Instead, it seemed to wrap around her and comfort her, like Papa's large arms.

In that moment, Manda knew she would never again need a light to quiet her fears. Now, with eyes opened or closed, she could dream her dreams. The Texans had won their battle, and so had she.

Three days later, Papa and Michael sat astride their horses, anxious to leave. The Tanners had invited the whole family to a party to celebrate the new freedom of the Republic of Texas.

Papa called, "Let's get going! Charles said to come early and stay late."

When Mama, Manda, and Padrac came out of the

house, they wore the same clothes they had worn the day they left town in such a hurry. Although Mama had soaked and washed the clothes, the material still showed stains from the mud they had walked through. But Manda looked pretty in her old pink bonnet with her blond braids beneath it, and her face beamed with happiness.

It would be a while before the family could replace what they had lost. The stores in town had also been looted, and goods would have to be brought in from Louisiana.

But the Barkers considered themselves fortunate. Many people came back to burned homes and had to camp out or stay with neighbors until they could re-build.

Before she climbed in the wagon, Manda put Happy in his pen and told him goodbye as she had always done. "I'll be back," she called to him as they drove away.

Then her mind turned to Jane. Manda had not seen her since they got back to Nacogdoches. She wondered how Jane would act—if she had changed after all they had been through.

When they arrived at the Tanner farm, Manda jumped from the wagon before it came to a complete stop. She ran to join the group of girls under the tall pine trees. Jane and two younger girls had already begun to rake the straw into lines.

"Hello, Manda," Jane said. "We're going to build the best house ever. I'm glad you're here."

"Well, thank you," Manda said, surprised at Jane's politeness. "It's good to get to play again."

After a while, the girls grew tired of adding rooms, so one of them said, "Let's go pick wildflowers to put in our house. I see plenty in that patch over there."

On the way, they passed by the field where Terror grazed. Manda glanced at Jane. Jane looked at Manda and grinned. They were both remembering the day Jane had teased the bull and barely escaped. Now that day seemed a long time ago.

The ladies all brought food and laid out a delicious meal, in spite of neglected gardens and empty smoke-houses. After supper, Papa and Mr. Nolan played their fiddles and sang "Old Joe Clark."

As twilight fell, Dr. Tanner called some square dances. A huge, round moon appeared over the tops of the pines. To Manda, it looked like gleaming, orange velvet.

Late that night, the Barker family left for home. Padrac fell asleep as soon as he got still. Manda lay quietly in the back of the wagon, looking up at the sky. The moon, now high in the heavens, had turned to silver. Millions of stars twinkled.

Manda stared at one of the stars. Because it glowed much brighter than the rest, it seemed closer. She thought, "That star must shine only in Texas."

About the Author

Martha Tannery Jones was born in Nacogdoches, Texas, on property once owned by Sam Houston. The land was given to Houston after the Battle of San Jacinto. She has been fascinated with the story of the Runaway Scrape since childhood when she was first told that her great-great grandmother took part in it.

During her research, Mrs. Jones discovered several accounts of the Runaway Scrape. Most of the information contained copies of original manuscripts or letters written by witnesses who described this event. Another account of the incident was recorded in the memoirs of a woman whose mother fled Nacogdoches and told her daughter of the experience.

Mrs. Jones and her husband have four daughters and live in Conroe, Texas, where she has taught school for twenty-six years.